FOR THE UNNAMED

(Black Jockey Who Rode the Winning Steed in the Race Between Pico's Sarco and Sepulveda's Black Swan in Los Angeles, in 1852)

Fred D'Aguiar was born in London of Guyanese parents, and grew up in Guyana before returning to London for his secondary and tertiary education. He has lived in the US since the mid-1990s and currently he is Professor of English at UCLA. He trained as a psychiatric nurse before reading African and Caribbean Studies at the University of Kent, Canterbury. He was Judith E. Wilson Fellow at Cambridge University and has been shortlisted for the T.S. Eliot Prize. *For the Unnamed* (2023) is Fred D'Aguiar's fifth collection with Carcanet. His previous poetry book, *Letters to America* was a Poetry Book Society Winter Choice in 2020. Carcanet also published his nonfiction, *Year of Plagues* (2021).

For the Unnamed

FRED D'AGUIAR

CARCANET POETRY

First published in Great Britain in 2023 by
Carcanet
Alliance House, 30 Cross Street
Manchester, M2 7AQ
www.carcanet.co.uk

A CIP catalogue record for this book is
available from the British Library.

ISBN 978 1 80017 341 5

Book design by Andrew Latimer, Carcanet
Typesetting by LiteBook Prepress Services
Printed in Great Britain by SRP Ltd, Exeter, Devon

The publisher acknowledges financial
assistance from Arts Council England.

CONTENTS

For Dylan, Aniyah, Cruz & Erin

'There's no nowhere for something to become nothing.'
Alice Notley, *The Speak Angel Series*

CALL

We gather for him:
hundred-strong choir;
cathedral bell tongues;

dance troupe at traffic
lights break out on red
in the middle of the road;

stadium where beats
rock young, middle, old.
Bring him back from dead

too long, raise him, claim
him from some unknown
grave that kept him lost

in history, stranded outside
time, banned from his name.

CALLING

Come back now for us
who need you more than
you should know or care

you seem big to us

time chained to your skin
stretched by our summons
fused to your good name

you cannot be us

your cord blood for ours
if we find your name
buried in your time

if you answer us

from your bed of skin
made by history
for us to sleep in

that keeps us awake

CALLED

Black jockey, stranger,
walks into a saloon,
heads turn, jaws drop
for no reason other
than your black skin.

You, nameless, strange
to us as much as to your
self in time, even if back
then you knew who
you were and did not

care if people called you
bad names, spat, cursed.
We bring you back to name
you, not for yourself,
you're way past caring.

You're here for us, as all
History must be if served
half-eaten for one group
while others starve fed
crumbs after a feast.

Dead, you ask us living
nothing. We need you,
fetched from ground
blessed by your bones
hungry for this light.

CALL, CALLING, CALLED

If we can name him then no one can blame
him for the glaring omission by his times.
Name him and we save him from attempts
to erase him from History that framed him.

He jockeyed Black Swan, rider and horse won
against wild favorite, Sarco, owned by Pico.
Poor Sarco, earmarked for victory, foxtrotted
through training, brushed more than pushed.

By contrast, Black Jockey worked Black Swan
in secret, at night, hidden in stables by day.
What the crowd saw made them gasp twice:
once at Black Jockey, twice, at thoroughbred.

Sweet fortunes placed on Sarco turned sour.
Token bets on Black Swan made sweet fortunes.
Newsmakers, why fail to name the Black Jockey
who championed Black Swan for Sepulveda?

Is Mansa Musa too much? Or conqueror
Abu Bakr II? Or magical Prester John?
His face on a coin, his name sung by choir,
his horse and him on a plinth in a square.

March, 20th, 1852, Los Angeles, California,
Black jockey no one saw fit to name,
won the biggest race in the west of that era,
start of a black tradition riding thoroughbreds.

If we could see him in some lucky audience
with the long gone and unjustly dead
this is what we would tell him, given the chance
to set things straight and bring him peace:

Forget that they failed to record your name
or accord you proper fame and reward;
feel the free power of a horse at full pelt;
be the one who shared that freedom;

keep it in your heart for the rest of your days
no matter they refused to grant you your name.
We name you now to right back then to put
to rest their hurt that saw you as stock.

We see you. Say your name. What you did brought
your horse fame, and left you as a mere footnote.
You ride once more with your name in the thoughts
of your audience, who see you and the horse; both.

You lead by seventy-five yards at the finish line,
and the victors toast the horse and both your names,
and the losers curse you and your fame and blame
your skill for their ruin, not the horse for winning.

B. J.

You make me feel like a borrowed library book
somebody never bothered to return to its nook.
The date stamped on me is so old, I'm appalled;
the library went South, pulled down for a mall.

You found that book, found me, in a thrift store
or at a droll country fair antique books seller.
Now you want to give me what's overdue, more
apt for your time than mine, you want to settle

scores in poetry that yards of newspaper columns
about the greatest race, failed to do in prose:
grant me dignity by saying my name with an art
that's all feel, touch, communion with a horse.

It's so long after my time, I do and don't, care if
you name me, keep it simple, not double-barrel,
for I was never one for airs, never quarreled,
I lived to race, lucky to have the ride of my life.

Do what you have to do to satisfy your time;
make sure you return me to my proper place
in history; check that people can say the name
you pick for me. I do not want to lose face

with my friends who will joke if they think
it funny. Where we remain, there's no end
to what we say, what we do, and no ink
that lasts long enough to make amends.

ETHEL

How do we carve out room to love
our life crowded with fending off
elbows?

You ask as we hold hands under
water after we stripped each other
bare

We sit on river bed stones
up to our necks in current hands
grip

More to steady ourselves we lie
barefaced fail to hide this found
trouble

Against all odds laid by our time
when black skin counts as work
stock

Worse off than pedigree horse
just above pigs, sheep, cows, or
bulls

If you take our labour as plow
pulled soil turned us pushed by
whips

Our hands tight against this tide
washed by currents that sweep clean
through

B. J.

This stream makes my skin feel new
Turns your brown lips two shades bluer

I feel weightless in it as if our love
Lifts our history off my back

And us off our feet so that we float
In a stream outside our time

If I can trust our love as the thing
That makes this stream pull and push and sing

Do not let go of my hand
Everything that I know lasts

As long as you keep my grip in this stream
That we bathe each other in

ETHEL

Not the light of the moon
But the moon by whose light
We count our luck in stars

Not the call of the caribou
But the caribou in each of us
That calls for the other

Not the burn of midnight oil
But midnight's oil on our skin
Burned as we clashed in bed

We cast long shadows around
Our walk and hands held talk
Shadows that melt under us

If time reads as our shadows
It passeth not for our love

*

Once or twice in life
Love strikes your spine
Straightens curves at top
And tail into lightning rod
For fingertips tongue touch
By one or two though never
Both at the same time for this
Love not just sex this what
Flesh thirsts for more
Than breath even
More than death
Equals free

ETHEL & B. J.

Does my belly show?
Your belly shows.
Am I getting fat?
You've gained necessary weight.
Do you still love me?
I love you twice as much for what you carry for both of us.
But do you still want me?
You have to ask? Look at us naked every chance we get.
What if you fall for another?
I would be out of my mind. Have a doctor check my head
and heart.
You have an answer for everything I say.
[pause]
Don't you?
[pause]
Don't pretend that you don't.

B. J. & ETHEL

Come here.
What, here?
Yes, here.
Now?
Yes, now. Unless you think it's a bad...
I want you.
I can't get enough of you.
One day you'll regret that you said that.
Let's not waste valuable time waiting for that day.

B. J. LOOKS BACK

In my game if I glance
round it's to catch how
much more dust I need
raise to blind the field
trailing in my wake.

I may have been beside
a river in a charitable
little tent when I fell
out my mother, grabbed
my first, hungry breath.

I dreamed of a palace
on a hill overlooking sea,
full ships docking riches,
jumping fish, handed me
spoon-fed, gold platter.

Or a farm deep in country,
fenced by forest, stream,
mountain, no barbed wire
or weapons, wheat, grain,
sky heavy with fruit,

blues so sweet, sad that
deep, cut I welcomed,
neck bared for warm
blade of that flood
swept me up, off.

I'm told I looked small
for my age, quick, strong,
show me anything once
I would show it back
at twice the speed.

I moved all the time,
walked fast with a bounce.
Nicknamed, 'Hurry up man.'
What I know from that time
confined to skull kicked

by a horse I whipped
on a ride in a bad mood.
That horse waited for me
to pass behind it and bang,
me out cold for two days.

I woke without my name
or my past, I learned from
what they told me about
our plantation and cabin,
that someone owned me.

I swore to buy myself
for my sanity, took horse
kick as sense knocked
into me to take notice
of my escape ticket.

I prayed for speed,
horse brought power.
I asked for strength
horse snorted, pawed,
nodded, shook.

Horse let me stand
in stirrups as I held
on for my life, until
we crossed line after
finish line, first.

DANCING SALT WATER

More of the life of a man on the run
Less of his sins from his time with a gun

If you know better then you be the one
To judge if what I did you would have done

Don't say one word just think it through
What in this time is a person to do

Surrounded by folk who buy up and out sell
Humans as stock seen as two-thirds people

Land that whites cleared with cannon and rifle
By picking off tribes while waving a bible

God's chosen on earth to spread civilization
Among ungrateful primitive first nations

All of my words channeled through me
None of what I say sorry for history

I live as I must if I want to survive
It's easy to say different when not in my shoe

I side with the winners against my own tribe
I act my part to train what they find wild

JOYCE

Need I remind you DSW who
Showed their most private parts,
Kicked by a horse you crossed
The wrong way, for me to rub
Aloe Vera and you to groan
At first that turned to moans?

Didn't I stitch you moccasins
That drew compliments every
Time you stepped out in them
On account of your initials,
In bold red on leather dyed
Black, colors of our tribe?

Was I the one who said there could be
None other walking this earth like me?

DANCING SALT WATER

I hold no words for what you do for me
Except to say that what you feel
If a stream bumping with salmon

I would add all the salmon from every stream
For more flesh of my love for you to move
As that current than water to carry my love.

If this sky that holds both sun and moon
At once this morning that wakes us
I would make room in that sky for all

Stars from last night rubbed out
By daylight for that sky filled so
Says no less that what I feel for you

No more than I can hold on my own
Without your love to help me now.

SALOON ONE

LA, where drinks flow, brawls spill from bars,
spewing into pissy streets, to fill jails with dumb farts,

paused for the work week only to gear up for Friday,
Saturday, more of LA with too much wild in its west.

1852 is a country half-formed, one eye on the Pacific
and the other, cast by pulp fictions, over the Atlantic,

about a nation still on the make, those times in backrooms,
boardrooms, smoked-filled, drink-swilled drawing rooms

on the take, the shakedown, handout, under the table deals
that left out enslaved, indentured and indigenous appeals

for a fair share, slice, shot, free, restored First Nation,
land big enough to share and not war over for some auction

dictated by superior weapons, when beaches comb and peal
from Santa Barbara, Malibu, Santa Monica, Venice, Seal,

Manhattan to Long Beach and beyond, where waves curl
their invitations to us to dip our toes, nay, plunge, hurl

ourselves into their embrace as they line up offshore
to come at us full speed with a steam train's roar.

This Indian, that Indian of my dreams, fishing with bare hands or, fishing with spear, walks up to me as I stroll in the street. Looks nothing like my figment: him in moccasins in his triangle house with his oblong horse and triangle spouse. Walks, head held high. Wears a gabardine suit. Waves a cane to match his steps, big waves, like a ringmaster in a stadium.

I pipe up with, I hear you can feed a wild horse corn from your hand and make the fiercest among them understand you when you speak. Bar talk says that you float about town like a ghost, that horses pause what they're doing to stare and nod.

You pay no mind to animals around you as if you're blind to the fact that they see someone who belongs to their kind. Give back to them. Train for me.

Hear me out. I've a race to win and a pedigree. All I lack is a trainer to teach that creature how to run the best race. Not flat out from the word, *go*, but measured, holding something back for the home stretch. On any track all my jockey has to do is stay out of the way of my horse.

Give me the win I deserve over a pompous opponent and his crew of hangers on. They eat his every word. Help me make him and them eat his small fortune of a wager against me.

My Black Swan's the best, all the way from Australia where he won everything. He's raw with talent. Regal is his middle name. He knows. It's not the rider or the race, it's that left to himself he would squander all that God-given grace. Help me to train him, as only you can.

DANCING SALT WATER

Stop, or not. Dig yourself in a latrine pit
you cannot crawl out. What you bark merely
adds to the echo in my breeches after a plate of beans.

> First, if I train a horse, I bring my rider, or this
> conversation's a nonstarter. He's small

for a man but he sits on a horse like an outcrop of it,
and rides as if in that horse skin. To see him, you'd think,
nothing to see here. Wrong. He's more gifted than me.

There's no trainer in this land that can make you win
Your race, without him. I don't care what you've brought,
nor from how far; not when you face a talent like Pico's Sarco.

> Second, show me your horse, if I like what I see
> I'll bring my rider and we start on the spot.

Third, call me, DSW. I'm Tongva. I live in a cabin
outside town. I am married. My wife's the shape
of our love and it's none of your business.

I don't train horses for them to make men money.
I work with horses to help find what they did not know
they had in them. The place of a horse is with the herd

> on a plain, not in your stable. Knowing that,
> I say, horse, I'm sorry for what I must ask.

Lend me an ounce of your ten-pound heart.
On your back I feel this volcano on the brink,
or river current left to boil, about to burst four banks:

> two that hem the river, a third upended
> in the blue for all to see, and a fourth in my
> head.

My jockey who works with me feels the same way.
He speaks for me in a race both of us have to ride.
He thinks like me as I would ride for him.

> He looks slight; don't be fooled; he has plenty
> upstairs and down. He's a beast at this game.

You'll never forget his name. And when you win
you'll love him as I do and want him next to you
to face whatever odds the world slings at you.

SEPULVEDA

I cannot wait to meet this prodigy of yours,
Kelly. Word says he keeps a woman
or she keeps him sane for his work.

DANCING SALT WATER

Tongues will wag. He is a jockey first
and a lover second. Though you're right
about his constant companion.
You hire me and him; you get the two of them.

SEPULVEDA

Will she bring trouble to my stables?
My men's tongues loosen after two drinks.
He won't fight for her honour or shit like that, will he?

DANCING SALT WATER

Oh, he will. So school your boys to mind their
tongues around her as they would if she were
your lady. Fair?

SEPULVEDA

Very.

CALL, CALLING, CALLED

This is where you
get your full name
match your race fame
make history yours

no fanfare of drums
procession of dancers
released white doves
or shaman canticle

just weeds of words
gathered by hook
dipped into a sea
folded like a book

with you lost there
until we fish you out
for a second look
at what history took

for too long gone
and so as good as
dead with nothing
left and nothing said

B. J.

In my dreams I fly across deep blue
on the back of a horse with wings

for hoofs and all I have to do is hold
on for dear life, breathe at this speed.

We leave sparks in our wake seen as
shooting stars; we rest as moon is to

earth as fish is to sea so horse is to me.
I ride for a life horse makes worthwhile.

DANCING SALT WATER

You speak for me in what you do
as a jockey. You know my mind
after a decade together. Set aside
your own thoughts and feelings.

Take on what your horse feels.
In a race, you and your horse
blend: the same thing made twice
as good when you act together.

You know all this and yet I must
say it to remind myself and you
why we do this and love it so much
that we take insults from rich

people just to keep doing our jobs.
I prefer a horse to most Whites.
They walk with guns and rule
with guns and guns make

their names, otherwise they
would be nothing and nowhere.
Only as wise as their guns, which
think for them. Money

runs through their veins.
They emit a gunpowder stink.
Do not trust the flint of their eyes
They look at us but don't see

Their equal. We see through them.
My friend, you're the best at what
you do, I know, still I have to say:
Check the shoes on your horse.

Keep them new but with some wear.
No one wants to wear new shoes
for too long though hoof shields
must be worn-in to feel comfortable.

Make it so that the new shoes fit
as if they were old favorites, make it
so that if you wake with them on
you feel nothing, clad in air.

*

As for you, horse. I say what I must
even if I know you might not listen.

Do I need to bite those hard ears of yours?
Make you accept what you already know, horse?

Should I use spurs to direct the traffic of my
thinking so that it sinks into your skull?

Are you the kind of animal who understands
only one forked tongue? The spur and whip?

I didn't think so. We'll get along.
It's your race to lose if you do

exactly what I say as you dictate
victory to me. Who's in charge? The bee

that roams between flowers or the honey
colors that pull that bee from one rose

to another? Neither one or other, more
both. Tell me what you need me to do

for you to profit from it, for things turn
out as we dream them or they shame us

dead. I've always time for a horse.
You move so fast you leave time stranded.

You make me forget how little time
remains up to me; how much I want it to end.

I prefer a victory parade to dribbling
braced in a rocking chair counting

on somebody to wipe my face and bum,
or tell me who I no longer am to my face.

BLACK SWAN

Let's swap
        you be the horse and I'll be the man
we take this race with you running on your hands

with me riding you as your mind in me and you as my hoofs
folded up in the air
                that's how easy this race comes off

for us
        though we tell no one that we talked and made
this pact to swap places with a look of nothing strange

except that a Black man sits in the saddle and stirrup
and a horse from Downunder
                runs the right way up

    *

We bread and butter-up empty plates, sweeten

sour faces with you on my back to turn hoofs fleet

through this city that I kick into faces with a beat

horse steps drum into dirt so the hardest hearts leap

at the sight us two cut flying past as never before seen

in LA, horse and human with the same black sheen

whip held by you more for its feel that pushes me

dig deeper in our joint quest for horse-man glory

SALOON TWO

Be well my friend be true act good
We have one life so live it well
You know a lie when you see one
Disguised in frills to turn your head
Think twice act once for good or ill
The time is gone to just sit still
And watch the world roll by and miss
The gifts that life offers for free
If each of us decides to pick
The rose that each moment presents
Such as a race with odds you can't
Make up they are that good so grab
A gift under your nose or lose
This chance life sent your way for free
You know we speak a truth so plain
You might mistake it for a lie
Flowers cannot fool you my friend
You see colours you smell a rose
The name fastens upon your nose
Even if doubt tells you not to
Trust what you sense must be a fact
We do not speak idly or waste
Breath on things best left alone
This pure breed Pico owns is
A joy to see train and compete
Sarco will win this race asleep
Sepulveda must know Black Swan
Stands no chance in a fair fight
Just lay your best bet here with us
Sepulveda will pay with his ruin
We hear he trains his horse at night

SARCO

Ours is the kind of race that could be run in half
The time around the village of Stockton or Town
Of Sacramento: one small, the other middling,
Places you don't want to find yourself at night
Stranded, unless you have a rifle and a friend
To watch your steed – bless them for their civic
Feistiness as they wish to grow up fast, join LA
And San Fran, in matching, city ribaldry.
It's 1852 and the nation has much growing to do.

Who can blame the west for seeing itself as the rim
Where every human impulse spills over and finds
Expression, and the slate of being human is wiped
Clean for a fresh start at being somebody, anybody
Worth their salt or better still weight in gold?
(That rush comes later.) I'm a horse able to gallop
Ahead of my bodily existence and see what's ahead
More than I look back, it's a horse thing not to
Check as you leave the competition in the dust.

Grab or steal may not be bad if
  Who you rob from does not know it
    Rather view you sent to save them
      Thank you they say bled by what you
        Do for them so they believe and
          Who are you to pull the wool off
            Them for your exposure as a
              Thief of their time spent blindfolded
                Sense by sense overloaded anyway
                  Fighting for survival day to
                    Day never mind this distraction
                      Brought by Sarco and Black Swan
                        Welcome though it must be seen as
                      Take what you can while you can is
                    Rule one rule two rule three you get
                  Where this goes so jump on board
                Now or find yourself left on the dock
              Watching the craft of our era
            Sail out to sea leaving you stranded
          Surely you want more than loss as
        Your sole ledger in this little life
      Given us to make of it what we
    Can in as short a time as possible
  Is what flesh says to all our dreams
Deathbed awake wishes included.

JOYCE

Man must lie in bed he made
or so I think until I hold him
in that bed unable to let him
go back to the life he made
for himself with no mind
for me in his arms as I am
and must remain until
some end comes our way
made by him that two of us
must carry joined as we are
no matter the condition
we find ourselves in as
designed by one of us for
both of us to inherit

either that or I walk
away back to my days
beside a stream with a hill
looking down at me
from a safe distance

back to my heart at a pace
I do not feel and take
for granted

versus this quick
pulse of life with him
living in a kind of sin
as his bible puts it
for what we do.

I think I stand in the middle
of a stream that divides
around my feet.

I see him as that water
fresh against his salt
tears shed for his lot
and mine in a time
not ours that we must
make it through or
flounder as the salmon
must think as they drive
between my feet

I spear the ones
within reach and keep
eyes to my side for a bear
that may want my perch
for the best of this season
driving upstream

man walks like he owns
where his foot lands
in a world ruled by whites
who need his touch
with horses to work
for them in their quest
to own everything
their eyes land on

I wish my stare took
in all there is to see
rather than thank
my stars for the sight

I wish my body moved
like the salmon at my
feet up and far from
where I was born
beside this stream
under a hill with no
apparent care one
way or the other for me.

MOON ONE

Count yourselves charmed
I cover ground you walk

I bathe your skin
Silver glaze your eyes

Liquid light my way
Behind your eyelids

Under your tongues
Nails between blinks

So that what I do
Stands for what you think

By you I mean all things
Bi-peds, quadrupeds hills

Valleys town city lake rivers
Even the wide-mouth sea

BLACK SWAN

I run from history, more, tiptoe,
into futures with me always first.
I've seen others draw carriages
around tidy, mini, Sacramento.
I crossed myself, Lord, don't sentence
me to life drawing carriages in squares.

When I sprint it's from the harness
of a cart, coach or carriage, the three-C's
for bad horses that spell equestrian Hell,
that dotty cantor disguised as a gallop,
hay in a bag after the flick of the whip,
shoes fitted by a drunk with one eye

on a bottle, barrel, or fucking butt,
(should that be firkin, you wonder?)
the three-B's of another kind of hell
for a riderless horse or a horse with no
shoes, feet worn to the bone, put to
pasture with old, tangled-wool mutton.

Give me this life of being combed down
after an evening training, wide-eyed,
my own roomy pigsty in the tidy stable,
and my rider and me in a pact for only one
outcome – pure and simple victory over
all comers. What kind of name is Sarco?

You'll never hear it again after I'm done.
I, meaning we, train in the dark so no one
sees our black skin trembling with effort,
nor the Black man poised on my back

to absorb my gallop, nor me at my best,
building muscle for glory and history.

It's a raceless thing, this rider and me
at this time in a race-baiting history.
It's a love thing if love is what we do
as we train at night and sleep days,
and stay close to one another and eat
the same corn that he peels off the stalk

for me, though I eat ten times more.
I paw the ground with my lead hoof
when he appears to tell him I'm ready
for whatever, whenever, test he brings.
He nods with everything in his look
for me to catch and do with as I will.

Do what? Win for the two of us, yes;
triumph over the weeks at sea to get here,
barely making it off that ship where I could
not keep anything down for long and my legs
turned to straw and I started to think a watery
grave was the design the stars patterned for me

When I read that bright upstairs as boundless
if my body sprouted wings and flew me up
to be the horse that raced across the sky
each night to land by morning in a stable
full of corn and mares (no rest for the devil,
or too devilish to rest; my shooting star wish!).

                *

My first whiff of him, I stared down my nose bridge
At his small feet and way over his head to grant

Him the height he lacked. He looked like he stood
Sideways as he faced me, he seemed that thin, short
And blacker than my black skin (which was the sweet
Part of meeting him). Back home I met Aborigines,
Black, people, as sniffed out by a black horse.

But here I thought a white boy would ride me
As the prize that cost my owner a tidy sum.
So as the jockey stood in front of me, I neighed
In delight at what I took to be a joke and harrumphed
As if to say, very funny, nice one, now come on,
Introduce me to my real rider? And when no one
Else materialized and he stood there and held out
His hand to pat my head I almost bit off his paw
At the apparent insult and obvious lack of seriousness
About the race of the century between Sarco and me.

Take this thing seriously, I said, eyebrows raised
Look cast at my trainer, and a dust-raising snort
That I directed at the Black jockey. Do not insult
Me with defeat miles before the race, by matching
Me with this slight excuse for a man (nothing to do
With his royal Black backside and everything to do
With how small he seemed and meek for a man
Meant to steer me to victory).
                                        As he held out
His steady hand I almost snapped it off –
Rotten carrot on a flimsy stick, bone plate
Offering to make me mad – but for something
In his lined palm that said this race was mine
To run and guide him and not for him to rule
Me from start to finish; nor me as muscle under
His commanding whip. I read, stubborn sod,
In dark lines on his brown and pinkish palm

(Pink from the scrub of handling a rope, I guess,
With blood, one color for all, a rose glazed with skin).
He offered himself to me in that gesture.
I kept my big teeth to myself, once I caught
What he meant. I turned my head away from him
To say that I was not that easy to placate, that he
Would have to win my confidence, earn it, granted
I was the horse and he the man – a switch I would
Have to make and convince him it was worth
Making for the sake of winning the race, and a deal
He might be open to in that open-handed gesture
Of his at our first introduction.
                              First, he walked
Beside me. Next, he ran with me, as much as he
Could keep up with his skinny legs and narrow chest,
As I cantered, more sauntered along to allow for his pace.
Then he sat on me in the stable and combed me
Busily as if he thought I might buck and send
His meek frame flying into the rafters, or worse out
The top of the roof for him to land, flat, in the yard.
I sent him a message through my black skin to his.
The message said, Do not fear me, Black man, I mean
You no harm. We have a race to win and there's only
One way to win it.
                  At this point I felt this quiz in his
Interest, through his skin; him asking me, how, in static
Jumping from him to me. I said straight out what
We must do to secure this victory of the century.

I felt his question surge at me through his skin:
What should we do to get this guaranteed win?
I told him. I spat it out, I did not care one iota for
A gentler way. "I become you and you become me."
He staggered and held onto me. "Steady," I neighed.

"It's not that bad. I may be a horse but I have more
Sense than most of your kind and though you're a man
You seem able to shift your shape from your slight
Frame to my fire box, steam engine power of a train."
(No modest way to phrase what I embody in my prime).
He asked, "I become you and you become me?"
                                                    I nodded,
Neighed and stamped twice for emphasis.
I become you and you become me. I told him to lean
In close, closer, so close, I could bite off his left ear,
And I whispered the whole, spell-binding enterprise,
Dreamed up as I stargazed on my voyage across the seas
From Australia to the ramshackle port of Los Angeles.
Wasn't it always the case that every living creature who
Ventured this far west had better nurse a big dream
To power them away from everything they know?

Well, I sailed over an ocean and lost so much muscle
In the hold as I vomited on empty and lost my legs
To land, that I had to remake myself, reinvent me,
From head to toe with just this dream of a big win
To see me through. Add this Black man with the slight
Frame to jockey me along to victory and our pact
Just between us, kept from my buyer and our trainer,
Since my jockey was free (said he bought himself back
For himself – what a way to put it) with his winnings
In St Louis (wherever that is on the map). Lucky you,
I said to him, to know what it means to run free,
When all I do is run for another and revel in their
Pride in me, as my pride, that though I am not free
I sail along and feel what it means to be free as I win
For my owner, earn my keep and pride of place
Among his stock and trade. Am I making sense?

That a horse while on the run in a race gets a taste
Of what my Black jockey said he bought for himself?
That the two of us know the same thing from opposite
Ends of the equation or different sides of the same coin
That chance throws up to see which side comes down
And in what time, and here we are in the middle of a
Century bound to it by convention, and ready to buck
Whatever that restriction means, even if it kills us.

That is how I run a race: I break from the start
Line and dig the ground until I cannot feel dirt
And air flows around me as if I beat wings, not feet.
No jockey. Not this Black man from a faraway land,
Just like me, he sailed, or his ancestors, I say him
Since he dreams that voyage nightly and thanks
His lucky stars that he never ended up in the drink
As so many like him, and me, who find the journey
Too much and long for the stars, enough to take
Flight from this body. But I speak for him when he
Should tell you in his way what he makes of all this.

B. J.

What makes you think I'm not serious? My size? My skin?
Same as Blacks, bought and sold in most of this land,
Worked until we out earn the right to buy ourselves
Back for ourselves to be free, or dream it and wake sour
In bondage to morning sun spread in cotton or cane fields
Burning us as we labor. I thought you might understand
More than most and yet you question my seriousness?
Is my grave without my name not enough of a price?

It is one thing to buy my freedom and walk this land,
But quite another to ride a horse at full pelt and feel
The same land sail under us, fooled into thinking
My horse sprung wings and I'm as free as an eagle.
This second freedom is worth more than the first,
Even as I fail to quench my thirst for emancipation
Of my people, and bench it, for this other hunger,
With you as my partner in our race of the century.

Let's settle all this talk about my below-average frame.
How would you fare if my weight doubled, at another
Foot and a half? I know you have muscle and enough
Will for a herd, but even you would feel flummoxed
By that handsome, bigger version of me on your back.
Take my diminutive frame as my gift to you. And keep
That picture of the giant version of me as my personality.
I may be small but I dream as big as you and fight as hard.

If I become you and you become me. you would know
My life, born into slavery. What a privilege for a horse!
Welcome to days on the run from slave catchers, dreams
To cross the Atlantic in reverse, untangle knots of tides,
Turn my life on this continent to free among equals,
Break the chains of my people. I see my life as a horse.
You as me and me as you, one being mixed from two.
Aware of despair, we keep a smile, a touch of style,

Crumbs, we eat the same corn, you prefer hay,
I can't stomach that though I chew bits of it
To settle my stomach and keep my teeth clean.
Did I just confess that? You make me speak

My mind like only Ethel can. Not even your
Trainer, my longtime friend, Dancing Salt Water,
Knows this about me: that my jockey ambition
Is second to none, Ethel and my race included.

BLACK SWAN

And you get to eat hay, walk on all fours and carry
All and sundry on your back. Folk see you and want
A taste or better feel of your power between their legs,
If I may phrase it the way people declare when they sit

On my back and I gallop for them and my pace travels
Up my legs and spreads through my body and they feel
This charge of my muscles like no feeling they've known
Bigger than the best of their lives, big as anything asleep.

They dismount, giddy, knock-kneed, brimful, as they take
A part of me with them under their skin, in their muscle,
That travels to their hearts and minds and instructs them
I believe, about horses joined to humans, one inseparable

From the other, bonded by a current that keeps our lives
Afloat until they bet on a horse and switch to seeing us
As easy money, ditching wisdom about us and them
If my hide, hoofs, mane trust me to win this game.

*

You know different. You're a man who feels what
It means to be viewed as stock. Your people, bought,
Sold and worked as stock, die with no name other
Than their owners, and no markers for graves besides
Temporary plots in a fiction whose sole kingdom is
Heaven after earth forced on them till they love.

Do not get me wrong. I think the spirit is a real thing.
Forgive me if I view the Black church as an offshoot
Of White people owning Blacks and calling them stock.
I may be a horse and stock but they call me Black Swan.
What's your name? Show me one White who knows it?
I'll show you a land of whites who do not care one bit.

B. J.

To hell with your thinking like a man. What do you know
About the benefits of worship? You eat, exercise, sleep,
Mate (if we let you loose in a field or stall with a mare)
And die if you break a limb and rarely end up retired
In the wild. What do you know about the inner life?

I see you fast asleep with your hoof flicking and I know
Your dreams are all about your engine on train tracks
Heading for the horizon, always heading with no mind
For a drink unless we lead you to it and even then
We can't make you drink and you seem as if you may
Or may not bother with water and just run yourself
Into the grave if we let you and do not make you rest.

When this race is won I want myself back from you
And we go our separate ways, you hear? You go too
Far when you put me down as stock, the same as you.
It took all my winnings to buy me back from my owner.
And all the time I knew he had no right to own me

And with that knowledge I had to live each day
As stock or perish if I rebelled with no where to run
And set up a life of freedom and no weapons to match
His, only my will to make him see that I was as good
As him and he was no different from me, and the god
That he gave me to keep me in my place that I made my
Own as I remembered religion from across the ocean.

B. J. & BLACK SWAN

*

Are we fighting here?

*

You bet!

*

We're using my-skin-to-your-skin shimmy to bicker?

*

If that's all you can do with me is say how much
I'm like you for being stock and enslaved, then, yes,
Damn right it's a fight!

*

Well, I may just shut down this system between us
And revert to my neighs and your tongue clicking
As a forum for our communication.

*

Or you can drop your superior haughty horse
Matches man demeanor and focus on the task
Of winning against Pico's spoiled steed.

*

Okay; truce?

*

Shake on it – fist to hoof.

*

I feel a song coming on.

*

Me too.

*

Shall we?

*

Go for it.

MOON TWO

I say I when I mean we
I speak for the sun
who lost their tongue
or deigns to speak
when this human run
at time on earth is done
which should not be long
as the crow flies
as the earth turns
in its star urn

B. J.

We're horse and human unified
a lover couldn't separate us
nor a butcher with their best knife

We're the shape of our twoness
become one in a flat-out sprint
you have to look close to see two

heads on one body with the whisk
of a tail and the fan of dirt kicked
up in our wake and sound of a herd

stampeding through LA town
cleared for our blind passage
if our force-ripe plan bears fruit

Edible since we're not in it
For money nor pride nor glory
not now that we know how

we must become each other
run from how others see us
if we're to be true to ourselves

BLACK SWAN

I'll run my heart out for you

Run myself into the ground

Make you feel what birds must

Surrounded by flying air

Change your status from

Human into a shape

People take for a horse

With wings and an angel

A Black angel on my back

Spurring me faster, higher

B. J.

My Ethel will be jealous to hear

    you say that, hear this reply:

        I'll ride like my life depended

            on it and never sit in the saddle

                and only use my whip to signal

                our need for a bit more speed,

            a tap for down, a slap for up.

        and lots of both from me

    to tell you give it everything,

leave nothing in your firebox.

BLACK SWAN

Let us dance in a field
With no fence, run
ruled by wind to rainbow's end.

Fall's mist rises in cloud drifts.
We splash in such crystal:
horse and rider and trainer.

Three creatures horsing around.
What would a spy think?
Wish I could join them?

Thought the night would coat
Black Swan's progress from the leggy, skinny
Scrawny thing, that disembarked at LA's port
After two weeks at sea, to the fattened, uppity
Fuck of a beast that thundered in the dark.

That a spy sent by Pico would see zilch,
Hear what might be mistaken for thunder
Rolling in from the sea or San Gabriel mulch.
Not this horse turned into a winged creature
From the gods above that someone filched.

As for the Black jockey – he was supernumerary,
A bonus feature, a distraction, almost décor
Or an extension of the thoroughbred's contrary
Black skin. Was there ever a horse to say more
About? Black Swan runs like he's on the prairie.

Coming second, losing, anything short of first
Place is tantamount to disgrace – that's Black
Swan's demeanor, and why with his thirst
He wins this race tomorrow, despite the fact
Of Sarco's pedigree, favored by a huge purse,

And his perfect record, no health troubles,
Seeming a sure bet especially after
The sight of an emaciated Black Swan wobble
Down the gangplank because Sepulveda
Wanted his horse to be seen on its cobbled

Feet, not lifted off the merchant ship.
Witnesses laughed at what they saw.
All bets flowed for Sarco as a hot tip.
Black Swan at one hundred to one was
A long shot for a horse to seem worth it.

Add a Black jockey, while he might match
The horse in look, he's sure to be a hamper.
Sepulveda argues that's the trick, to catch
Folk off guard with the look of an amateur,
A Black, and make them think he'd hatched

Plot over one too many in one of two saloons,
Lull Pico not to pay mind to his need to train
Sarco and take the race in his stride as won
Before it's run, who, for rider hires a big man
Too heavy, too savvy to rise before noon.

BLACK JOCKEY & BLACK SWAN

How many countries you know
That have deserts and forests
And mountain ranges topped
With snow and more rivers than
Names we can think of for them?

*

America. (Should that be plural?)

*

Australia, mate.

*

We have more to lose.

*

We're a continent onto ourselves, mate.
You still want to argue the difference?

*

Why do you always have to win?

*

Ask me that after the race and see how you feel about it.
It's getting dark let's get on with training.

It's never the same thing twice and every time
I see it I think it twice as nice – how dark thickens

As if added to a pot of light left to simmer.

                *

God spare us – a thoroughbred and a poet.

I've checked the course for potholes; clear.
I've scouted the perimeter for Pico's spies; clear.

We've got someone ready to take your times.
We're watched closely by Sepulveda so smarten up.

                *

Then we're ready and may as well wear blindfolds
For what we must do. You want me to sprint in the dark.

                *

Not just you. Us. There's no you or me, remember.
We're conjoined and as scrambled as two creatures can be.
I for you and you for me and our twoness besting either one.

                *

Listen to yourself, preaching what I taught you.
Now I can play as hard as a man and you can think
Like a horse on the run from a wanted poster.

There's a bounty on my head in this race.
I intend to collect it for myself by winning.
You know that if we lose you do not get to walk.

There's a crowd with so much bet on me
That if we lose they'll lynch you. The worse
That can happen to me is cut loose as a stray

And that's not as bad as you think. I won't starve.
I've seen herds of wild folk like me just roaming.
I can join them and blend in and forget my past.

You on the other hand have nowhere to run
And nowhere to hide, not for long, and no disguise
Fit for a man you size and obvious color.

       *

I wish I could take your talk as concern and not a poke
To get me started on another argument. Time's wasting.
I'll take you up on that lack of disguise thing later.
It's clear that you see my skin as a sin whereas for me
It's a blessing since I know where I came from
And I know where I'm heading. And I love Ethel.

You're a horse, not a man. Remember that. You say
You can roam with the wild herd but how far
Will you get before a rifle singles you out, or a rope
Lassoes you and a saddle shackles your back?

I can find my passage over the sea.

       *

I have Australia. If I win this thing I book
My passage home in some shape or form.

       *

The only way you're getting back Downunder
Is as part of a chariot team crossing the heavens.

I notice in all your speculation there's no option
For the two of us sticking together to the end.

That after all this we might go on to bigger
And brighter things as a team. How come?

*

Because people can never be trusted
with the life of a horse or bird or fish

Because your kind see yourselves as above
every other life form not counting God

Money and more money's your religion
blinkers most things and stifles language

Love of life tied to endless profit
in a life without love outside purchase

Don't get me started on your kind

I don't number you among them
on account of your skin

You belong to a church of just one
skin peeled for raceless flesh and blood

*

Thank you.

*

De nada.

*

You're speaking Spanish now.
Will you ever be able to find your way
Back to being a horse after this is over?

*

Maybe I won't be alone. Who knows?

*

Did you just wink at me?

*

I did. And didn't you feel me nudge you as well?

*

I did. A nudge and wink
From you, is more than enough
For me to take this race as the start
Of history made by us.

*

Shall we train?

*

Yes, let's.

*

As if our lives depend on it.

*

You bet.

*

Hold on tight my jockey, between our black skin and this
Night, you can't tell who's who as I sprint through dark
That blindfolds both of us, so I put all my trust
In your check of each inch of this ground for potholes
I mean sticks and those stones my ankles roll and twist
On or worse trip and break one of my golden legs.

*

You can guess how I feel in this dark, that's supposed
To hide how good you look from Pico's spies,
Should something go wrong by accident or design.
My life hangs on how well I comb your training ground
On my hands and knees as I sweep it clean of scraps,
On your back as you sprint makes me just as fragile
If you tripped, so I pray through practice and beyond.

*

I pray to Pegasus.

*

I pray to Legba

*

May our drills in the dark keep us safe, make us strong.

*

May we run with night eyes, discern what's good from harm.

*

Did I tell you the one about the race that I ran
In the opposite direction to the rest of the field?

Gravity turned me around, spun my head,
For a while I had no idea what I was doing.

Though I'm not the horse I once was
I can pack a lot into my shoes, if the right

Rider points me in the correct direction.
Yep, once I ran the wrong way in a race.

Let's say I was puzzled by my jockey:
Whose only skill was to issue strings of curses

As he tugged on my reins and dug into me
With his spurs and whipped me nonstop,

When all he had to say to me was turn.
It's hard to find a neat fit between

A horse and rider, yet it's as important
As a correct fitting of my shoes

To be paired with a good jockey.
I've had my share of bad ones

Who sit on you and you can tell
In a stroke that they don't have a clue

What to do with so much at their fingertips.
I glanced left and right and concluded

I was racing all on my lonesome.
I thought maybe I'd left the pack

In a few bold strides, but people were pointing
Like they do at a sight for sore eyes

And they were in hysterics, then I looked back
Only to see the receding rears of my fellow steers

Bouncing away in a flurry of loose soil,
My competition, almost out of reach.

I saw red. I turned and ran my shoes off.
My rider lost his hat and whip trying

To hold onto me. He clutched my neck.
Soon I reeled in the pack, caught them,

Started to overtake them one by one.
Who knows what would have happened,

If the track did not run out. Another horse won,
But my performance was the talk of the town.

*

You were the horse I dreamed about flying,
when I prayed to be America's best at riding.

As a child I climbed a tall oak, edged out on
a limb, crouched, held by thighs for as long

as I could stand the farts, slash of my vanity,
gasp and not fall, and wonder about my sanity.

You glowed in my mind as that limb in that tree,
your gallop for this breeze, your back under me

holding on, as I urge you go faster for that winged
feel, not feet, for feathers, not bare, animal skin,

run from my hunters, from those who see me
as obedient, pure labour for free,

that no good comes out of the children of Ham,
brought from a primitive, faraway, empty land.

So I jockey, to escape what they do to black
people in this land, to keep whites off my back,

to feel fully human on a horse at full stride,
not just fulfilled but brimful with pride.

DANCING SALT WATER

Let us stop our moonlight runs
shadows harder than our real selves
cast in silver and stretched
over our training ground.

rest now that we did
all that's to be done to win
your two minds act as one
twin bodies combined

our rest earned by how
hard we trained at night
harder than our shadows
cut by this close moon

BLACK SWAN

One day before the big race.

How did we get here so fast?

Times I looked at the sun

Impatient for it to set so we could train.

Now they comb and brush me

For my final night at ease.

All the talk about how much rides

On my victory makes me nervous,

Not about the race but about what

It must be like to place all your holdings

On one event with so many things

That can go wrong and so much

Left to chance.

*

I look up – we both do,
As the evening drops, a silk scarf
Pitched from a heavenly balcony,
Or a parachute, adrift, its strings cut

From the weight of the day,
That day loose from its moorings
Drifts out to a blackened Pacific
Pegged to the night sky.

*

Hummingbird rips past
In a flurry, amid dusk's liquidity,
Its gold in puddles plastered impossibly
Sideways, on walls, trees,

Hummingbird, flee to your haven
After your last pick of a flower's purse.
You fly backwards, upside down,
(Might you be Australian?)

Faster than detonations of wings
That happen so fast they join
A stream of displaced air
In your wake, winged space,

Where you stick in mid-air,
Stitch space to this vacuum,
Where your wings blend,
Turn feathers to stone.

Hummingbird gone before
Its noun fastens on my tongue,
(That should say our)
I count my jockey as me.

Bird faster than thought.
Both of us thinking this
Before either of us could say it
And so neither one bothering

To state the obvious,
Reading each other's mind
In a dry run of tomorrow's race,
Hummingbird taking Sarco's place.

Except my rider takes the bird
For American and I claim
It for Australia, our only partition
Between two joined bodies.

                    *

We offer joined prayers
To space between dusk and night,
That turns our limbs into wings:
May we be that hummingbird;

May we make light work of Sarco
Tomorrow, grab the fat purses,
All those bets against us,
Black jockey and Black Swan.

                    *

I look at him and he
Returns my stare,

As if my sight, aimed at him,
Reels him in to look at me.

What is there to say
That training over a month

In the dark has not pinned
Down? Either that, or we turn

Up tomorrow, embarrass
Ourselves and ruin Sepulveda.

My jockey's way of hugging me
By the neck as if he plans

To hang from me and swing
Like a child, except his hug

Involves his entire body
And it takes over my whole neck.

All I have to do to reciprocate
Is shake my head in agreement

For him to bob up and down
And he bounces off me as quick,

As if a hug could only be stolen
From what's all business between us.

*

So much of what we did
We left unspoken, or we

Could not find words
For what happened before

Our eyes as muscle, nerves,
Something in our marrow

Summoned by our trainer
Drilling us through night,

Caught by us between wing
Beats Hummingbird sings

Outside time inside space
Under a fibrous moon.

Or we made magic of need,
Juju, luck, obeah for what

We knew we must do to win
Our right to our names.

Fasten to my mane, grab
With your thighs, trust me,

As I trust you, my better,
Other, more fragile half.

      *

We trained under a thick moon.
We waded through oceans of light.

We ran flat out as we hid from view,
Guided by a feel for earth in the dark.

What we must make in broad day
With eyes wide we take from night.

*

Name me a time and place
you find words fail you,
or you say something
smart without fail?

Is there ever a thing
that happens so fast
it slaps the words out
of your mouth,

Leaves your tongue
flat on your palate,
mouth blazing open
like a Venus fly trap?

*

Yes, you. The way you run as we hide.
The way I feel on your back, more luck

Than any one person should have
In a short life, more life thanks to that

Luck, more than I can bear and stay
Sane and be of use to you and us.

*

Don't go mad on me now, not so fast.
Thank you for the salute and praise.
Though I've yet to earn it in full.

Running in the dark with you is easy,
You carry yourself like an extension of me,
I read your thoughts from your skin to mine.

*

Until I met you I'd given up on being
Understood. I craved a mate but knew

That for a former slave such a thing
Was a long shot and vain hope.

The last thing on my mind was you;
A horse would understand me more.

I mean, mate, in the Australian sense.
I thought it would take a partner

To muster this level of intuition.
I did everything in America with my skin

At the front of me as the first thing
Everyone sees before they see me,

And since my skin has a low premium
In this land and at this time I did not

Expect to ever find another living soul
That might come close to knowing what

I think and feel and want from my life,
Least of all a horse from Australia.

*

Horse my ass! Thoroughbred to you,
My friend. If you want a horse look in
Any stable and at a herd on any plain.

I'm a different prospect, as you know
By now and as the world's about to find
Out tomorrow from us when we win.

*

I know a goodnight when I hear it.
Would you object if I slept near you?

We both need our beauty sleep
So we might as well stick together

With only the rest of the night
Left to ponder victory tomorrow.

*

By all means, just don't snore
Or I'll boot you out of here,
And I hope you don't talk

In your sleep, or fart for that
Matter. I'm a light sleeper.
The silent ones wake me

As well, with their smell,
So don't improvise in my
Vicinity, or on my account,

I need earplugs and blinkers.
You need as much as me for
This night to be one of peace.

*

I'll sleep like a stool. You won't hear
Squat out of me. I'll keep my dreams

Private and use the fact that I'm near
You to mull over our plan for tomorrow.

I can't believe this can happen here
And now won't let you out of my sight.

*

Sweet dreams, my friend.

*

Goodnight Black Swan.

MOON THREE

All I give you
Comes at a price
Paid by a bank
Stored in your sleep

    Polished shine
    Spring clean
    Air brushed
    Rain swept

All you do is take
Keep and don't share
Grab and hoard
Plunder and squander

    Polished shine
    Spring clean
    Air brushed
    Rain swept

Why I love you
Sun can say
None must know
Outside of love

    Polished shine
    Spring clean
    Air brushed
    Rain swept

*

They sleep light, under a Rota of guards
Set up by Sepulveda to cover his rear.
To lose the Black jockey would be hard

But all that he owns rests on Black Swan,
All his hopes for a jackpot and all his fears,
Not to go bankrupt, end up empty-handed.

In the morning his prized possession wins
If his Black jockey follows orders, grips reins.

Dancing Salt Water and Sepulveda lecture:
Spare the whip and you win the spoils.
Keep your feet in the stirrups, lock your

Eyes on the rocky road ahead. LA's
Streets leave nothing to imagine, soiled,
Dropped, thrown, planted pitfalls

By careless citizens who reserve civic
Pride of place for private spaces, public

Thoroughfares for someone else to care
About, the result a dumping ground
For things people don't want in their

(not-in-my-if-I-can-help-it) backyard,
That same unwanted thing (your pound
Of flesh) they think nothing to discard.

Broken furniture, slop from buckets, dead
Cats, dogs and anything you care to name

That somebody sees fit to pitch at your head,

As if when out for a walk they won't meet what
They threw out for someone else to claim,

Trip over, as if the street were a waste plot.
Running in the dark forces the runner to see
LA's streets in their mind's eye, like chi.

So the Chinese refer to what you have inside
That you turn outwards to avoid ruts and pits

That come at your life, one of them is pride,
The other may as well be our ambition.
Hoofs must touch all things with lightness,

Any fortune teller would say for nothing.
Or, be first to look before foot drops all its
Weight; as you know, a rock's brightness

Invites wise feet to roll, or twist and sprain,
Worse, break bones, that end all games.

If nothing yields to that initial light touch,
Meaning the coast is clear, the same step
Converts caution to abandon and digs much

Deeper into that same road for more speed.
Strapped for time tied to our gambling need
Is this bigger gamble by our blind all out

Sprint in streets we do not know and pray
We last nine miles of LA.

*

At Ranch Pico, the night is a brawl, drinks
Flow, ribaldry rules well into the small hours.
Bets rack up debts in anticipation of a big
Payday, winnings spent well before the break
Of day and start of that race, the running,
Viewed as a formality, meaning the party
May as well get going immediately, before,
During, and certainly after what's a formality:
LA, stamped on the racing map with Kentucky.

Two drunks wrestle to stay upright, one plays
Sarco by fighting with a hand behind his back,
The other is a reluctant Black Swan, handed
A knife to even the one-sided contest. Another
Two put a blindfold on one to level the scales,
With the sighted one as Swan, and the blind
One as the triumphant Sarco; even with this
Advantage, the mind of the fighters, geared
On behalf of the underdog, end up losing.

No Rooms For Rent anywhere in the center.
People from as far as New York, Florida,
Pockets full, curious to see what the west
With its land's-end feel for finality
And its new as new can be sense of need
For approval, can do to match the rest
Of the country where most questions
Were settled with just one question left:
What to do about slaves who enrich a nation?

*

At Sepulveda's place, all is quiet as if calm
Were a palliative for a win, or some balm
(Assuming the calm brewed and grew it)
Spread on all life on that ranch, principally
Black Swan who wanted no one bragging
Or showing jitters, just assurance of a win
That would come as a shock to everyone
Outside the inner circle, all that secret
Training in the dark, lips sealed, bets

Held back till the last minute, an air
Of caution someone seeing it might
Read as misery faced with the inevitable.
Sepulveda told his jockey what to do,
Keep in touch with the frontrunner
Until the last mile, hold back Black
Swan who loves nothing more than
To run all out from start to finish,
Eight furlongs out let Black Swan go.

You grow an air of calm in a house
By taking the doors off their hinges,
By having everyone wear a muzzle,
And by wrapping all the noisy metal
Objects such as pots, pans and ladles
In bandages, everyone walks barefoot
The only scratching is from birds nesting
In the eaves that someone failed to inform.
The watchdogs stifle barks, whines and growls.

*

Hold on if you can Black jockey
At no point do you see one of my hoofs
Touching the ground all of me airborne

And my body at a stretch just out of reach
Of the second hand of a clock and so
Out of touch with time therefore

Beyond the measure of distance, duration
Or anything that is not in this dream
Of the thoroughbred that I am in full

Flight with you on my back though
I hardly feel a thing since you're small
For an adult and who can tell if

You're there in the dark that joins
Your Black skin to mine and to night
Made for a dream like this hours

Before I prove what you and I know
To a crowd of disbelieving eyes
And dropped jaws come morning.

*

I feel your eyes on me so I keep still

When I really want to turn over

Switch sides and nestle deep

Into another dream carriage

Pulled by a sleep engine

Fired by my ambition

To win everything I do

Every time I enter a race

There's only me to lose against

As long as I have legs to run and run

Left in me I'll win or hang up my spurs

*

Trying not to sound like headlines
From a history lesson,
I turn to good, old, reliable insults:

Sir, you're a tomato left out too long
In the sun. A watermelon
In the desert. Manure, that soap can't cure.

*

I've known some cruel owners
Who live by the whip and use the lash
In place of speech.

I've seen a horse
Bite back and leave a brand of its teeth
In the bone of a man's shoulder.

*

I'm one of the lucky ones, born
To parents who bought themselves
Back from owners who wanted nothing
More to do with them given their talk
About one race under God's sun.

*

We sing the same song,
Human, horse, animal, mineral;
Both seen as profitable stock;
Both young, gifted and black.

*

When I crane my neck at night,
I see herds grazing in the sky:

Sparks of found life whose time
Never runs out. Sometimes one

Gallops with winged feet across
The face of that occupied field,

In a final time-fling, and is gone,
Granting my wish to join them.

When I race it's with or against
The revolutions of our sole earth,

Rather than opposite another,
Or for some bounty, or boast.

In every race I'm on both sides,
For and against, win, or lose.

*

You mount my back
you whip my flank
I ride my best
to win for us
I see the course
before the start
up close, hoof by
hoof by nostrils
that sniff furlongs

to feel my way
around pitfalls
that throw us all.

This track or field
or road invites
lose or win,
legends begin
or die quick in
sands that house
blind ambition.
One of these two
results when you
enter this race.
Blow on your dice,
throw with a spin,
gamble implies
a game for kicks,
not this journey
to save your life.

ETHEL

He says he's all mine
yet he sleeps with a horse
between us.

I know he's there
by the alarming way
he cracks his fingers.

Just when I think
he doesn't care
if I'm there or not

he reaches over Black
Swan and grabs my hand
and cracks my fingers.

I whisper, No. Stop. Don't.
I try to pull away,
but he keeps cracking

and I love the feeling.
I offer him my other hand.
He takes his time to crack

each joint in each finger
and a warm tingle
swarms lips, tits and hips.

I invite him to crawl over
Black Swan's sleeping bulk
or the horse feigns sleep

as we move slow and keep
our breathing even trying
not to wake the thoroughbred.

We press our faces
cheek to cheek,
lips next to ears,

arms locked around
each other holding
on in what seems

smooth rafting for now,
for the rapids we feel
coming just ahead.

My flesh becomes ears
for what he says;
his flesh all ears for me.

Ethel, he says, Ethel,
Under his quick breath.
Yes, Jeremiah, yes.

Our backs buckle,
our hipbones crack;
skulls flint sparks

under mixed breaths;
Ethel, Ethel, Ethel;
Jeremiah, yes, yes.

*

A Mediterranean morning lands in LA:
Light strokes from the sun sowed by breeze
Off the Pacific that mops the dew off blades
Of grass, the milk moustache off a calf.

Wood shutters swing open fast and on time
And for those who partied through the night
Today starts with a deliberate drag of its feet,
With wads of time to spend and an audience.

Folk put down poles and buckets to mark
Their spot as they grab a bite or a bathroom
Break or they tip a lad to hold their spot
By the road as they top up their bets.

The air among people carries this current
So that everyone is giddy and impatient
At once and want this race to be over
Already so they can party with their win.

It's the kind of ready that does not need
A starter's gun, the start of something
Underway before it properly begins,
The way history feels as it's being made.

*

Sepulveda tells Black Swan to make him
Proud and add a bundle to his fortune.
He tells the Black jockey to hold on tight
And keep out of the way of his thorough
Bred, no whip no spurs no speech nothing.

Let the horse think for itself and do what
It was born to do and shock everyone.
Just stay on the back of the beast was all
The jockey had to do, just let the horse go.
And one last thing, enjoy the ride of your life.

Sepulveda called the Black jockey by a name
Not given to the press or given but left out
By reporters bruised by the surprise result.
Or it may be the scissors of History bent
On cutting Black people out of its annals.

The ride into town by train festooned
Everybody with jittery nerves, sweat,
What if, maybe, that spawned doubt,
Dried saliva in mouths, stilled tongues.
Sepulveda outstared steam into space.

Prayers as never before. Lucky charms
In case supplications fell on walls of wax.
Consult cards, leaf, palm and star readers,
For the day to fall in their favour, placate
Gods of sport, chance and good fortune.

*

Black Swan felt all their nerves and fed off
Them as a foot feeds off the ground for traction
As eyes roll over things to fasten their names.

The Black jockey stuck close to the horse as if
Touch were all he needed to keep Black Swan
From losing and touch was all he could trust.

What was left to say that had not been said
Dozens of times with the doing? The drills,
The feeds, the brushes, the shoes, no mating.

A look said more and no one could see it
Traded between horse and jockey, or if seen
No one would know what it meant to the two.

So with a touch here and a look now and then
And a touch there, the two had a conversation
Nobody could hear and it settled their nerves.

They picked up on the giddy air, those currents
Desperate people send, that if picked up shocks
You into a similar state of wobbly, weak knees.

A lightness that travels from the head down
To the stomach and a brashness that's costly
If it translates into a bet rather than stillness.

You don't need a clairvoyant to tell them
Their jittery and garbled speech, with a fine
Tremor in the hands and a sweat moustache

Where none should be – all point to the need
For the wise to sit down and leave running
Around to those who can't help themselves,

The ones who float like corks on water
Bobbing with every little twist in the tide,
Who end up washed up choking a gutter.

ETHEL & JOYCE

I, we, countless times what we loved
fell before our eyes, against our will

I, we, fold with them, die their deaths
only to return strapped to memory.

Theirs is the release granted by dying.
I, we, stay for their loss as our sole gain.

Mobs stormed our streets, our homes,
hiding places, over and again, I, we,

relive each street, house, hideout.
We beg, curse, strike back, fall.

I, we, after all the soil we tilled,
clothes scrubbed, meals cobbled,

mines dug, herds gathered, infants
nursed, shoes reheeled for them,

still, they come, we fight, we fall.
Take some of them with us to hell.

We left dirt for this promised gold.
I, we, give flesh, blood, how long

some forget, misplace in songs,
feet up, smoke pipe, grow old

*

Both sides of the road lined six-deep,
People squashed, spilled over balconies,
Children clambered up trees, hung on limbs
If their parents didn't push them through
To the front telling them to beg pardon
As they sidled for a ringside view.

Press everywhere, owners and horses.
Trainers and jockeys, left and right
Of the start where a referee coddles
His start-gun and other judges assist
The ref if anything crops up that needs
Adjudication, or whose side are you on.

If you could bake, you made quick sales,
If you mixed sugar and water and hops
You pedaled unguent to lift spirits people
Lined up for in their long wait in the street
That became the weight of their thirst,
If anticipation could ever be a nerve.

The sun climbed for a better view,
The breeze circled with pickpocket ease.
Marshals made a show of their badges,
Shouting at anyone who crossed the street,
Touching their hats with a nod at women

Poker-faced in head-turning fineries.

Sarco

I'm built to win, you're built to come in second. Get used to seeing my behind.
From the day I born I showered in success. How can you spoil that for me? No. Look around you. See how many uprights have staked their life earnings on my victory over you. By running against me you pit your hopes against destiny.

Black Swan

From the horse's mouth to your gods of predestination, I offer this:
a game of chance, this gamble between us means your destiny must take a back seat. Forget the crowds in your favor, think about your honor if you beat me fair and square. Or lose. There's no shame in either outcome for horses of our pedigree.

Sarco

Strip all this attention. Drop the wager. Cut the two of us loose on a plain or savannah away from prying eyes. I see the same result: you on my tail and the gap widening between us the longer we run. I dream myself at the head of every herd, not in your company in some unworkable equality of the animal kingdom.

Black Swan

You don't budge an inch in your boasting. In the race that we have to run you will be the horse that runs its heart out for glory. With talk like that, if I happen out front, pulling away, at the end, you will run yourself to death hoping to catch me.

Is that how things end? Thoroughbreds primed
At the start, trainers pulling reins to steady them
Side-by-side, to face the crowd-fenced street
For stretched seconds cut loose with a bang?

Folk laugh at the Black jockey and show surprise
At the condition of Black Swan. Sarco's rider
Looks twice as big as the Black jockey, matches
Pico's confidence in Sarco. But Black Swan....

The talk's less brash. The shine on him.
Bets, already placed, the odds stay at one
Hundred to one against Black Swan and his
Black jockey, mounted on a horse to meet

The rules of a rider needed for it to be a race.
Head scratch, head shake at the Black jockey.
Thigh-slapping laughs. Some hack and mash
The spit into the ground at the sight of a Black.

Curse Sepulveda for smearing the occasion
By his choice that makes them look twice:
Once at the improved horse, twice at the Black
Astride it; and if there's time for a third eyeing

It's with regret at not placing a bigger bet
Given those odds, sealed by this Black joker.
All praise Pico for his average joe on Sarco,
The two look caught on an afternoon stroll.

Now the starter lifts his right arm freezing
The snorts and stamps of the horses, eyes
Train on the spot. Bang! Folk jump, pigeons
Scatter, two thoroughbreds rear, spring.

QUADRILLE FOR THE UNNAMED

Call, Calling, Called as D. S. W.

A liddy-biddy person of our own
trained to ride a unicorn
bareback: kiss, kiss

Moon & Saloon as Joyce

You bite the cord
I'll make her latch
onto me: what, no kiss?

Call, Calling, Called as D. S. W.

Someone with your goods and my savvy
as you call my work with horse,
jockey and turf: kiss, kiss

Moon & Saloon as Joyce

She must cook and sew,
sure, but hunt, kill,
cure and dance too: what, no kiss?

Call, Calling, Called as D. S. W.

First thing, I'll count the toes.
second, fingers, see if a sixth
passed down: kiss, kiss

Moon & Saloon as Joyce

I'll dye her skin,
braid her hair,
colors of our tribe: what, no kiss?

Call, Calling, Called as D. S. W.

Handed down my line to me,
mine, cut off, before I knew
what from where, along
with the hood of my ding-a-ling: kiss, kiss

Moon & Saloon as Joyce

Up to the point of her first
bleed, she belongs to us;
afterwards, she's mine: what, no kiss?

Call, Calling, Called as D. S. W.

I name him; you name her.
If both, we pick together.
He or she or they will need
company: kiss, kiss

Moon & Saloon as Joyce

I know in my bones
that I carry a girl
or boy, who may as well
be one: what, no kiss?

Call, Calling, Called as D. S. W.

Let's have fun making more,
as with your crafts and my training:
not life but living is the thing. Kiss, kiss

Moon & Saloon as Joyce

I'm all for fun and games
even when I craft my arts
and work with you at our love: what, no kiss?

FOR THE UNNAMED

come to us showing bare
palms scored with lifelines
lived on behalf of the drowned.

Speak to us through sealed lips
stitched by needles wielded
from their time to our standard,

we hear groans, screams, pleads,
see veins stand on foreheads,
necks, temples, threaded in eyes,

understand that for us to move
we must tread on their bodies,
three-deep in places, yielding.

Accept that we breathe for them,
air taken from them, speak as
them with our unsealed mouths

if this chant counts for anything
our slogans, our fists strike
air, our feet stamp songs.

NAMES

Some for outdoors, some for in
Some for us in the heat of loving

Some for kitchens, some for fields
Some for bathing, some for wells

Names for our shields
Names for our dances

Names for breaking fasts
Names for raising dead

Names for a toast
A boast, a ghost

Names for chapter
Play and verse

All these names for all these places
So many sounds to go with faces

All for us when we meet all of them
Morning, noon, night and in our dreams

Won't you? Shall we?
If not now, when?

B. J. & ETHEL

You know you're on the verge of breaking my fingers, don't you, dear.

A crack is nowhere near a break, my love.

Keep going. You know what you're doing, dear.

Each joint in your fingers adds up to our years together, my love.

Has it been that long since our days in the stream, dear?

What you call a stream was the winding neck of a river, my love.

My brain is a sieve when you start on my fingers, dear.

Are we still up for this life in the middle of nowhere, my love?

It's the middle of everything we've ever wanted, dear.

You're right. Wild herds. Fields of corn and wheat. A river, my love.

Our house that we keep adding to for our sprawling life, dear.

You're the one who collects everything, my love.

I only do it because of the interest you take in everything, dear.

I wonder what Black Swan is up to now, my love.

Australia is huge, dear.

It needs to be for a horse with his ambition, my love.

Do you regret not going with him, dear?

No. Black Swan and I did what we were put on this earth to do together.
  Win, my love.

Yes, you two won big, dear.

Now I'm where I've always wanted to be, my love.

Me too, dear.

Call

What a picture those two make?!

Calling

Yes. All of them.

Called

You think he'll like his name?

Calling

Which one?

Called

Any of it; the whole shebang.

Calling

Hard to say. He strikes me as fussy.

Call

Rightfully so.

Called

Yeah, he can afford to be picky. [BEAT]
Do we qualify to name him?

Call

Only qualification is life.

Calling

It takes more than just life, surely.

Call

Who you calling Shirley? [NUDGES CALLING]
Add will, motivation.

Called

If I died without a name, I'd die.

Calling

Yep. Two deaths in one life.

Call

I'd haunt the fuck out of the living.

Calling

Maybe they're dead too in their lives.

Called

How so?

                                        Call
What does it take to deny someone their birthright?
                                        Calling
A really fucked-up person.
                                        Called
Or system.
                                        Call
Precisely; death in life.
                                        Called
Not life in death?
                                        Call
Now that you mention it, yes, both.
[PAUSE]
                                        Calling
What don't we know?
[PAUSE]
                                        Call
E=MC squared.
                                        Called
What will happen next week.
                                        Calling
I was never any good at equations or reading tea leaves.
                                        Called
What are we good for?
                                        Call
Naming the dead.
                                        Calling
They don't care.
                                        Called
What's the point?
                                        Call
For the living; for us; anyone who cares.
                                        Called
It's a thankless task.

Call

It's a privilege. We get to make peace with our ancestors.

Calling

That calls for a toast.

Call

Make it then.

Calling

You.

Called

[SPEAKS TO CALL]
Have a go.

Call

Ok.

[CALLING, OPENS BOTTLE. SPILLS A LITTLE TO
PLACATE THE SPIRITS. POURS THREE GENEROUS
GLASSES.]

Call

To Jeremiah Zebulon Jiawattikah Chukwe!

[THEY CHINK, STARE EACH OTHER IN THE EYES
AND DRINK. LIGHTS OUT.]

BLACK SWAN

Those days I narrowed my eyes, lowered my head, stretched my legs.
Breeze freed me from the grip of earth. I weighted next to nothing.
My skin listened for him on my back with his light touch of my reins.

His legs trembled towards the end. All that sweat made me worry he
would slip clean off me. I prayed he would hold on. He prayed I
would not falter and fade. Dancing Salt Water prayed for both of us.

Has LA seen anything like it since? I should know from where I sit
looking down on lives running into each other, not checking where
they run or so it seems from up here where we move without moving;

where the race is not to be won, nor even run, in a time outside of any
clock I know that measures these things, deep inside, my bones, I go
by my luck at my place among stars for all time known to the living.

I dream about our big race and about him as I fly in my condition of
thinking, always stretched across the sky at the head of a herd.